M000205470

# Resilience.

## How to Turn Adversity into Strength

Josh Floyd

RESILIENCE

An Hachette UK Company
www.hachette.co.uk

Vie Books, an imprint of Summersdale Publishers Ltd
Part of Octopus Publishing Group Limited
Carmelite House
50 Victoria Embankment
LONDON
EC4Y 0DZ

www.summersdale.com

Printed and bound in Malta

ISBN: 978-1-78685-966-2

Substantial discounts on bulk quantities of Summersdale books
are available to corporations, professional associations and other
organizations. For details contact general enquiries: telephone:
+44 (0) 1243 771107 or email: enquiries@summersdale.com.

# Introduction

Life has its ups and downs, and knowing how to adapt to adversity is essential to our health and happiness. Resilience is the ability to bounce back from the difficulties we all face. The good news is that psychologists have identified methods and strategies that enable us to navigate through crisis and overcome misfortune. This little book is packed with encouraging quotations and simple tips to help you build your inner strength and weather the tough times with hope and resolve.

# LOOK FOR THE SILVER LINING

Mentally strong people have the ability to see the positives in tough circumstances. Rather than seeing the world through rose-coloured glasses, they recognize that it's possible for good things to come from hardship. This doesn't erase the hardship, but it can make it easier to cope with. The next time you face a challenge, ask yourself, "What can I learn from this? What is this an opportunity for? How can this positively affect me?"

Every day you
may make progress.
Every step may
be fruitful.

Winston Churchill

# Make It a Habit

Mental toughness or "grit" can be cultivated. Think of it as a muscle that needs to be worked in order to grow stronger. To exercise your "grit muscle", push yourself in small ways on a daily basis. Resist the snooze button in the morning and get up and go for a run. Turn off the TV and write a paragraph of the book you've been saying for ages you want to write. Move the trickiest task to the top of your to-do list at work.

By practising mental toughness in tiny ways, you will prove to yourself over and over that you have what it takes. Mentally tough people are not more intelligent or talented than the average person; they're more consistent. Practise "grit" on a regular basis. Good things happen at the edge of your comfort zone.

WHEN YOU COME
TO A ROADBLOCK,
TAKE A DETOUR.

Mary Kay Ash

**However long the night, the dawn will break.**

African proverb

# Focus On Your Strengths

Many people base their sense of self-worth on external factors such as what others think of them or what job they do. As a result, their confidence is extremely unstable – an "off" remark or a bad day at work can cause their self-esteem to plummet. The key to resilience is to base your sense of self-worth on who you authentically are.

One way of doing this
is to identify and focus
on your unique strengths.
Think of a time when you
did something you were
really proud of. Now think
about the strengths, skills
and talents you used to
make this happen.

These are your signature
strengths. Know that
you carry these with you
wherever you go. You can
deploy these strengths
whenever you're faced
with a challenge, such as
moving home, starting
a new relationship or
changing career. Embracing
your strengths will give you
confidence in your ability to
handle any challenge that
comes your way.

There was never
a night or a problem
that could defeat
sunrise or hope.

Bernard Williams

# CHOOSE YOUR RESPONSE

We all experience bad days and crises in our lives, but how we respond to these situations is up to us. When something "bad" happens, we can choose to react negatively, or we can opt to remain calm and look for a solution. Often our reactions are habits we've fallen into. It's important to realize you always have a choice. When faced with a setback, pause for a moment and consciously decide how you would like to respond.

# FIND YOUR CALLING

A sense of purpose can enable
us to overcome challenges which
might otherwise overwhelm us. It
can give us the determination to
keep going, despite discomfort.
This is best summed up by a quote
from the philosopher Nietzsche:
"He who has a why to live can
bear almost any how." To find your
purpose, identify what you're drawn
to. Which moments make you
feel authentic, as if you are doing
something you were truly made for?

Perhaps you have experienced this feeling when organizing a charity event, nursing a sick animal, or creating a work of art. You may have also experienced "flow", which is a state in which you're so immersed in what you're doing that time seems to disappear. Look at what gives your life meaning and trust what your heart tells you. A strong sense of purpose will fill you with motivation and enthusiasm, and help you to transcend the ups and downs of life.

# Do not be embarrassed by your failures. Learn from them and start again.

Richard Branson

**The bamboo that bends is stronger than the oak that resists.**

Japanese proverb

# If at First You Don't Succeed...

It is continuous effort – not talent or intelligence – that holds the key to success in life. Successful people understand this. As a result, they are action-oriented. Of course, sometimes it makes sense to quit, but don't make the mistake of giving up too early. Walt Disney's first animation company went bankrupt and he was reputedly turned down 302 times before he got financing for creating Disneyland. Equally

J. K. Rowling was, in her own words, "as poor as possible" before she found success with Harry Potter, but only after 12 publishers rejected her manuscript.

Ask yourself, are you looking for a quick fix? Do you have a tendency to give up when things get tough? Or do you persevere and keep trying to find a way to make things work? Commit to keep going until you reach your goal

IF YOU LEARN
FROM DEFEAT,
YOU HAVEN'T
REALLY LOST.

Zig Ziglar

# THIS TOO SHALL PASS

When you're going through a tough time, it can feel as if things will never change. Perhaps you move to a new location, struggle to make friends, and think you will always be alone. Or your relationship ends and you feel as if the pain and heartache will never stop. Whatever the situation, remind yourself that "this too shall pass". What is stressful now will be just a memory within a few weeks, months or years. Nothing lasts forever. Everything changes with time, especially the way you see things.

WHILE WE MAY

LOSE HEART,

WE NEVER HAVE

TO LOSE HOPE.

H. JACKSON BROWN JR

**To persevere is important for everybody. Don't give up, don't give in. There's always an answer to everything.**

---

Louis Zamperini

# HELP SOMEONE ELSE

Volunteering can be a great way to distance yourself from your troubles. It will shift your focus from yourself to others and can help you put things into perspective. You could volunteer regularly at a food bank, or simply look for opportunities to help a neighbour, friend or colleague. Studies show that volunteering reduces depression, increases happiness and self-esteem, and boosts our sense of being in control of our lives.

**It's not that I'm so smart, it's just that I stay with problems longer.**

Albert Einstein

# What's Your Explanation?

---

The way you explain life's setbacks to yourself is important. Psychologists say that an optimistic (and therefore more resilient) "explanatory style" is composed of three main elements.

Firstly, optimistic people view the effects of bad events as being temporary rather than permanent. Secondly, resilient people don't let setbacks affect unrelated areas of their life. Finally, resilient people don't blame themselves when bad events occur. They see other people or circumstances as being the cause.

People with an optimistic explanatory style tend to be happier, healthier and more successful at work, school and in sport. Those with a pessimistic explanatory style are more prone to depression, anxiety and low self-esteem.

WHEN YOU HAVE
EXHAUSTED ALL
POSSIBILITIES,
REMEMBER THIS:
YOU HAVEN'T.

Thomas Edison

**Scar tissue is stronger than regular tissue. Realize the strength, move on.**

Henry Rollins

# PRACTISE GRATITUDE

Taking time to acknowledge what is good in your life can make all the difference when adversity strikes. Studies show that gratitude lifts our spirits and floods our body with feel-good hormones.

How you practise gratitude is up to you. You could end each day by reflecting on all the things that went well, or you could look for things that make you smile as you go about your day (such as an unexpected hug or bumping into an old friend). Some people find it useful to have a dedicated gratitude journal in which they write down three things they are grateful for every morning or evening.

By training your mind to notice what's right in life rather than what's wrong, you'll have more emotional strength reserves to tap into to help you bounce back from the stresses and strains of life.

Happiness is
a way of travel,
not a destination.

Roy M. Goodman

# EXTRAORDINARY LIVES

The bigger your dreams and goals, the more likely it is that you will face hurdles along the way. When this happens, will you give up or persevere? A simple way to strengthen your inner resolve is to read about other people who have overcome great odds. From famous figures such as Winston Churchill and Rosa Parks to lesser-known heroes throughout the arts and sciences, seek out true-life stories of courage and resilience and draw strength from their examples.

**Ever tried. Ever failed. No matter. Try again. Fail again. Fail better.**

Samuel Beckett

# Mastering others is strength. Mastering yourself is true power.

Lao Tzu

# Learn to Breathe

"Learning to breathe" sounds like a strange thing. After all, we breathe all the time without thinking about it. However, many of us take short, shallow breaths and, as a result, are depriving our bodies of much-needed oxygen. Breathing deeply nourishes our systems. It increases our energy and mental clarity, and it switches on the parasympathetic nervous system, which calms us.

The next time you encounter a stressful situation or realize you are feeling anxious, place your hand on your stomach and take a deep breath into your navel, letting your body relax and fill with air. Then exhale s-l-o-w-l-y. Repeat five times or until you feel calm. Several times throughout the day, tune in to your breathing. Is your stomach clenched? Are you taking shallow breaths from your chest? Are you holding your breath? If so, practise a few rounds of deep breathing. If done regularly, this will gently retrain your body to breathe correctly.

THERE ARE TWO
WAYS OF MEETING
DIFFICULTIES:
YOU ALTER THE
DIFFICULTIES
OR YOU ALTER
YOURSELF
MEETING THEM.

PHYLLIS BOTTOME

**All of us suffer difficulties in our lives. And if you say to yourself "find a way", you'll make it through.**

---

Diana Nyad

# The Power of Solitude

There is so much pressure to be active and busy that it can be hard to justify spending time alone "doing nothing". However, periods of solitude can play a crucial part in building your emotional resilience.

Time alone gives you a chance to stop and reflect. It allows you to tune in to who you are and what matters most to you. It encourages self-reliance and a feeling of being in the driving seat, rather than your life being controlled by external demands.

Try taking regular time out for solitude, even if it's only 5 minutes a day to begin with. Meditate for a few minutes in the morning, eat your lunch in the park, listen to soothing music, or sit by a fire and gaze into the flames. Make a point of setting aside time for rest and reflection and see how much better you feel.

The world
breaks everyone,
and afterward,
some are strong
at the broken
places.

Ernest Hemingway

# BE PART OF SOMETHING BIGGER

Spiritual beliefs can be a source of great strength in life. Whether you are religious or not, strengthening your connection to something bigger – such as God, nature or the universe – can both comfort and inspire you during dark times. Make time for contemplative practices such as prayer, meditation or spending time in nature. Studies show that people who are spiritual tend to be more emotionally resilient.

# CHANGE YOUR ABC

Many of us believe that negative events cause us to behave in a certain way, but research reveals that our reactions are based on our individual thoughts about adversity. This explains why people respond differently to the same stressful situation.

A person might experience adversity (A) in the form of their partner leaving them. They might then have the belief (B) that they are worthless. As a consequence (C), they would sink into despair and find it hard to summon the motivation to go out and meet new people. But another person in the same situation might recognize that their relationship hadn't been working for quite some time and that they are now free to meet someone who is right for them. They would feel sad about their relationship ending, but they would be optimistic about their future and decide to join some local clubs to widen their social circle.

Reflecting carefully on the ABCs in your life will help you overcome difficulties rather than letting them overwhelm you.

WITH ORDINARY
TALENT AND
EXTRAORDINARY
PERSEVERANCE,
ALL THINGS ARE
ATTAINABLE.

Thomas Fowell Buxton

It's the size of your hope
that's going to determine
how far you'll go in your life.

John Johnson

# Yogic Life

The benefits of yoga go far beyond improving physical flexibility. Yoga can help you sleep better. It can stabilize your mood and reduce stress and anxiety.

There are lots of different styles of yoga, which means there's a class to suit everybody. Hatha yoga (a generic term for "physical yoga practice") focuses on postures and breathing, including a short period of deep relaxation at the end of the class. Iyenger yoga emphasizes precise alignment and the use of props such as blocks, straps and belts. Kundalini yoga awakens energy in the spine through postures, meditation and mantras. And Ashtanga yoga is a strenuous series of flowing poses designed to build strength and endurance.

Whichever style you choose, regular yoga practice can help you embrace the present moment and find a feeling of peace, even in difficult situations.

**We must accept finite disappointment, but never lose infinite hope.**

Martin Luther King Jr

# If we believe that tomorrow will be better, we can bear a hardship today.

Thích Nhất Hạnh

# AFFIRM YOUR STRENGTH

As the saying goes, "What you think is what you become." A powerful way to boost your confidence and fortitude is to repeat affirmations of strength to yourself. Experiment with different statements until you find one that resonates with you. For example, "I am strong, whole and complete" or "I can face any challenge". Repeat your affirmation quietly or silently to yourself at intervals throughout the day and whenever you face a setback or difficulty.

# HOPE IS PATIENCE
# WITH THE LAMP LIT.

Tertullian

# Small Steps

When faced with
challenges in life, we
can become paralysed
with fear. Whether it's a
big challenge, such as
starting a new business,
or a small challenge,
such as starting a
fitness regime, the key
to success is to face the
fear and take action. The
easiest way to do this
is to take a small step.

Pick one thing you're currently procrastinating about and think of at least five ways to take a step in the right direction. For example, if your goal is to get fit, you could begin with the small step of doing one push-up or squat a day, or going for a 10-minute walk in your lunch break. Don't be put off by the size of the step. Small steps lead to big results over time. With each new step, your confidence and enthusiasm will grow. Keep moving toward your goal. Resilient people take action.

ONE MAY WALK
OVER THE HIGHEST
MOUNTAIN ONE
STEP AT A TIME.

JOHN WANAMAKER

**Difficulties are things that show a person what they are.**

Epictetus

# LET IT OUT

Honour your feelings and recognize that difficult emotions such as anger, depression and loneliness are a natural part of the human experience. Let your emotions out by having a good cry if you need to. Crying can help you to regain your emotional balance as it releases toxins that have built up in the body due to stress. You should find that you feel calmer and less anxious afterward. Another good way to express your feelings is through a creative outlet such as painting, blogging or playing a musical instrument. Creative activities can reduce stress and help you to process your experiences and feelings. The options for self-expression are endless. Whether you write poems, take photographs or draw sketches, creative pursuits offer you the space to deal with a range of emotions in a healthy and constructive way. Find something that gives you release.

IF THERE IS A SHIELD
OF FAITH THAT
YOU CAN KEEP UP
AGAINST DIFFICULTIES,
HUMOUR IS THE
TEFLON COATING.

Laurel Lea

**When you make a mistake, learn from it, pick yourself up and move on.**

Dave Pelzer

# VARIETY IS THE SPICE OF LIFE

If your days have a drudge-like quality to them, take a look at how much variety there is in your life.

Participating in a range of activities keeps your body and mind stimulated and healthy. A multidimensional life will also protect you from being knocked off course by a single setback. When you're living a rounded life, a "failure" in one area is less likely to demoralize you and make you feel like a failure overall.

You can't turn
back the clock,
but you can
wind it up again.

Bonnie Prudden

# Let Go of the Little Things

Nothing will sap your strength more than dwelling on things that don't matter. Worrying about a friend who doesn't reply to a text message, or the driver who cuts you off on your way to work, is a waste of valuable time, energy and brainpower. Obsessing over trivial things won't accomplish anything other than making you feel tired and irritable.

Save your energy for accomplishing what matters most – whether that's raising a loving family, running a successful business, or collecting money for a charitable cause. It will take conscious effort and practice, but you can train yourself to let go of the little things and focus your energy on the things you can control. Don't let negative energy weigh you down and prevent you from reaching your full potential.

**We must free ourselves of the hope that the sea will ever rest. We must learn to sail in high winds.**

Aristotle Onassis

# If you would know strength and patience, welcome the company of trees.

Hal Borland

# CREATIVE SOLUTIONS

If your path is blocked, create an alternative route. Creativity is your ultimate weapon. For example, if you want to meditate but "don't have time", practise mindfulness in the shower each morning. If you want to learn French but can't afford tuition, listen to an audio language lesson when you exercise. If you want to start saving but "can't afford it", start putting some money aside every month. Whenever you hit an obstacle, find a creative way to climb over it or go around it. Never let it stop you.

PATIENCE AND
PERSEVERANCE
HAVE A MAGICAL
EFFECT BEFOREWHICH
DIFFICULTIES
DISAPPEAR AND
OBSTACLES VANISH.

John Quincy Adams

KEEP THE FAITH,
DON'T LOSE YOUR
PERSEVERANCE
AND ALWAYS TRUST
YOUR GUT INSTINCT.

Paula Abdul

# CULTIVATE COMPASSION

When faced with a setback, it's all too easy to be hard on ourselves – but that won't help a bit. If you have one cigarette after quitting, or fail to stick to a new study regime, beating yourself up is likely to start a downward spiral that can be hard to escape. Instead, practise self-compassion. You actually made an effort, which is more than some people ever achieve. Treat yourself with kindness, climb back in the saddle, and keep going.

# Good Food, Good Mood

There is a strong connection between what you eat and how you feel. Eating a balanced diet will keep both your body and mind healthy.

Aim to eat plenty of wholefoods such as fruit and vegetables, meat and fish, and nuts and seeds. Avoid highly processed, packaged food and fast food. While it's tempting to turn to sugary food and refined carbohydrates such as bagels and pasta when times are tough, this will only make you feel lethargic and less able to deal with stress. Instead, choose foods which soothe and calm, such as avocados, Greek yoghurt, salmon, eggs, asparagus, blueberries, spinach, nuts and camomile tea.

Besides giving your body the nutrients it needs, making healthy dietary choices can help you feel positive and empowered.

WHEN THE WORLD
SAYS, "GIVE UP",
HOPE WHISPERS,
"TRY IT ONE
MORE TIME".

ANONYMOUS

**Whatever good things we build end up building us.**

Jim Rohn

I DON'T MEASURE A
MAN'S SUCCESS BY
HOW HIGH HE CLIMBS
BUT HOW HIGH
HE BOUNCES WHEN
HE HITS BOTTOM.

George S. Patton

# WHEN LIFE GIVES YOU LEMONS...

If you're stuck in a traffic jam on your way to work, how do you react? Do you accept the situation and take advantage of the extra time to listen to the radio, or do you tense up and sink into a bad mood? Whichever way you react, it won't change the situation. Resilient people make the most of whatever situation they find themselves in. In this way, a traffic jam becomes an opportunity rather than a waste of time.

YOU HAVE POWER
OVER YOUR MIND —
NOT OUTSIDE EVENTS.
REALIZE THIS, AND YOU
WILL FIND STRENGTH.

Marcus Aurelius

**Perseverance is not a long race; it is many short races one after the other.**

Walter Elliot

## HAVE AN ARGUMENT
## WITH YOURSELF

Just because you believe something, doesn't make it true. Many beliefs which we have held for years – often since childhood – sabotage our resilience. Start challenging the beliefs which are holding you back.

Psychologists recommend judging your beliefs on four criteria. Firstly, look at the evidence. Does it support or negate your belief? If your partner leaves you and you begin to question your worth, focus on the evidence that disputes this. Secondly, consider the alternatives. Rather than latching on to the bleakest explanation for a bad event, find a more positive explanation. Thirdly, what are the implications? When faced with a setback, try not to draw negative conclusions. And finally, think about usefulness. Question the utility of your beliefs – even the most negative situations can have hidden gifts in the end.

So, whenever you recognize beliefs that are holding you back, try replacing them with new, more empowering ones.

If you fall behind,
run faster. Never give
up, never surrender,
and rise up against
the odds.

Jesse Jackson

## LIGHTEN UP

Seeing the funny side of life can help you rise above painful situations. Don't assume a sense of humour is something you're born with, though. You can train your brain to see the lighter side. If you're struggling, take a step back in order to gain some perspective. Try not to take yourself too seriously. Note the absurd or ironic things that happen to you. A sense of humour won't cure all your problems, but it will make them a lot easier to deal with.

WE DON'T EVEN KNOW
HOW STRONG WE ARE
UNTIL WE ARE FORCED
TO BRING THAT HIDDEN
STRENGTH FORWARD.

Isabel Allende

# WORDS OF INSPIRATION

Sometimes a comforting or positive word is all we need to motivate us to keep going. Consider keeping a book of inspirational quotes on your bedside table or in your bag, so you can dip into it on a regular basis. You could also write out your favourite uplifting quotes and put them in your wallet or on a mirror where you can see them every day.

**Let perseverance be your engine and hope your fuel.**

H. Jackson Brown Jr

# Success seems to be largely a matter of hanging on after others have let go.

William Feather

# LOOK AT THE BIGGER PICTURE

When you're going through a rough patch, try going outside at night and gazing up in awe at the stars. Reflect on the fact that you are a tiny speck on a beautiful planet in a universe of 100 thousand million stars (that's "1" with 29 zeros after it!). Viewing your life as part of a bigger picture can put your problems into perspective.

IMAGINARY OBSTACLES ARE INSURMOUNTABLE. REAL ONES AREN'T.

BARBARA SHER

**Act as if what you do makes a difference. It does.**

William James

How wonderful it is
that nobody need wait
a single moment before
starting to improve
the world.

Anne Frank

# RETHINK STRESS

Begin to see stress as a professional athlete views his or her workout – as an opportunity to grow stronger. Stress builds character. It tests your resolve and problem-solving abilities. Look at it as a workout for your mind. Or turn it into a game and challenge yourself: how calmly can you steer through life, despite the bumps in the road? Viewing stress in a more positive light can help you embrace life's challenges and obstacles.

GREAT WORKS ARE
PERFORMED NOT BY
STRENGTH BUT BY
PERSEVERANCE.

Samuel Johnson

# Stop the What-ifs

When things go wrong it can be easy to let your thoughts run away with you. Constantly imagining the very worst possible scenario or outcome is something psychologists call "catastrophizing". For example, let's say you haven't hit your monthly sales target at work. This sets off a chain reaction of negative thinking in which you see yourself losing your job, going bankrupt, and your marriage breaking up.

As soon as you realize you are overreacting like this, take a step back from your thoughts. Challenge how logical they are. Does not hitting your sales target for one month really mean you will lose your job, marriage and financial security? Or is the reality that you have performed well in the past and there are things you can do next month to improve your sales?

Stopping yourself from catastrophizing takes a lot of conscious effort, but if you continually challenge your irrational thoughts, you will feel less demoralized and you will be motivated to take action to make things better.

THE CAVE YOU FEAR
TO ENTER HOLDS THE
TREASURE YOU SEEK.

Joseph Campbell

**Whether you think you can, or think you can't, you are right.**

Henry Ford

# Lessons in Failure

No one is immune to failure. We all experience disappointments, frustrations and bruised egos from time to time. However, resilient people don't let failure stop them. They find the lessons hidden within these difficult moments and use these to help them overcome their next challenge.

If you've made a mistake or something's gone disastrously wrong, take a little bit of time to reflect. Ask yourself some constructive questions. What did I do right? What could I have done better? What's the lesson here? Entrepreneurs, scientists, inventors and leaders all know there can be no success without failure. Most people experience catastrophes in some form or other, including financial problems, breakdowns and relationships ending. Successful souls manage to pick themselves up and persevere, armed with greater knowledge and wisdom.

**What lies behind us and what lies before us are tiny matters compared to what lies within us.**

Ralph Waldo Emerson

# In the middle of difficulty lies opportunity.

Albert Einstein

#  RATION YOUR WILLPOWER

Resilient people may seem to have superhuman willpower, but the truth is that they have learnt to use their willpower wisely. Research shows we each have a finite amount of willpower and it fades throughout the day. Each decision and act of self-control we make depletes willpower from our inner reserves. So if you spend the day juggling stressful tasks and suppressing the urge to shout at a colleague, it's no wonder you come home in the evening and give in to your sugar cravings.

The first step to maximizing your willpower is to look after yourself. Exercising regularly, eating healthily, and getting a good night's sleep will help to top up your energy levels. If you're hungry and tired, your self-discipline is more likely to falter. In addition to this, try not to take on too many things at once. Avoid being in a position where you need lots of drive and determination every day. Spread demanding tasks over several days and mix them up with less demanding ones. Using your willpower wisely will help to recharge your inner strength.

# BELIEVE IT!

When you adopt a new, empowering belief with absolute certainty, you can accomplish virtually anything. Here are four inspiring beliefs to try out:

- There is always a way if I'm committed.

- The past does not equal the future.

- There are no failures – only outcomes I can learn from.

- Everything happens for a reason. I create my own life.

Never give up,
for that is just the
place and time that
the tide will turn.

Harriet Beecher Stowe

# Expect Good Things

Our brains are wired to find the things we're looking for – so if you're always focusing on the negative and waiting for things to go wrong, your life will reflect that. The quickest way to recover from a setback is to tell yourself that things will get better. An optimistic outlook will lift your mood. It will motivate you to take action and persevere, which will drastically increase your chances of success.

As Winston Churchill famously said, "I'm an optimist. It does not seem too much use being anything else." From now on, focus on things going right. Try visualizing what you want, rather than worrying about what you fear. Envisaging the light at the end of the tunnel can fuel you with the strength to get through a tough patch.

ONCE YOU CHOOSE

HOPE, ANYTHING'S

POSSIBLE.

**CHRISTOPHER REEVE**

**The choice to have a great attitude is something that nobody or no circumstance can take from you.**

Zig Ziglar

# Warrior Body

It's easier to face adversity when you're feeling fit and strong. Take care of yourself by exercising regularly. Experts recommend around 30 minutes of physical activity each day.

Exercise helps build resilience in several ways: it produces endorphins and serotonin which lift your spirits, and it changes the way your brain responds to stress, making it more resistant to anxiety. It can also increase your energy, boost your confidence, and promote better sleep, all of which will help you to bounce back from stressful situations.

Any activity counts if it raises your heart rate and makes you breathe faster and feel warmer, whether it's brisk walking, dancing, rollerblading or swimming. Signing up for a team sport or exercise class, or exercising with a friend, can motivate you to stick with it and work harder. It also makes getting fit more fun!

IF WE ARE FACING IN
THE RIGHT DIRECTION,
ALL WE HAVE TO DO IS
KEEP ON WALKING.

Buddhist proverb

# Difficulties strengthen the mind, as labour does the body.

Seneca the Younger

# GO ON A MIND VACATION

Giving yourself a break from your busy mind can be restorative and healing. Mindful meditation is a practice which involves paying attention to the present moment and being aware of thoughts, accepting them without judgement. This helps us break out of habitual and often negative patterns of thinking.

You can learn mindfulness from books, CDs, online tutorials or classes. A simple way to get started is to sit quietly for a few minutes and close your eyes. Bring your awareness to your breathing. Focus on the rise and fall of your chest or stomach, or on the sensation of air going in and out of your nostrils. If your attention wavers and you realize you are lost in your thoughts, gently bring your attention back to the physical sensations of breathing. Avoid the tendency to label your thoughts and feelings as good or bad – simply let them go and return to your breathing.

After a few minutes, gently open your eyes and notice how you are feeling. Scientists say mindfulness can help us tolerate stress and deal with challenges more calmly and effectively.

**Don't be discouraged. It's often the last key in the bunch that opens the lock.**

Anonymous

# Fall seven times, stand up eight.

Japanese proverb

# Dear Diary

If your mind is swirling, spending some time putting your thoughts onto paper can help. People who regularly write in a diary or journal say that it calms them and helps them to emotionally process their day.

Expressive writing is also a great way to clear your mind and work through solutions your to problems. If you would like to try this, find a quiet time and place and write continuously for 15–20 minutes. Write quickly and try not to judge or censor your writing. You can write about your feelings, create a poem, or even jot down song lyrics to express your emotions. Your journaling will be most effective if you do it on a regular basis. Many people say that their diary quickly becomes a trusted companion.

WHEN WE LONG
FOR LIFE WITHOUT
DIFFICULTIES, REMIND
US THAT OAKS GROW
STRONG IN CONTRARY
WINDS AND DIAMONDS
ARE MADE UNDER
PRESSURE.

Peter Marshall

# REDIRECT YOUR MIND

Ruminating on worries and problems can trigger a downward spiral. If you find yourself replaying upsetting events in your mind or imagining horrible scenarios, try distracting yourself. Be careful which distraction you choose, though. Many people try to numb unpleasant thoughts and feelings by watching television, drinking alcohol or comfort eating. Healthier, more uplifting distractions include going to the gym, seeing a movie with friends, reading a positive book or heading out for a walk.

# Nature's Medicine

Make walking and being outside in nature a regular part of your routine. The fresh air, exercise and contact with nature are guaranteed to raise your spirits.

Studies show just 5 minutes in a green space can reduce blood pressure, and a 20- to 30-minute walk can have the same calming effect as a mild tranquilizer. A walk can also be a good way to get a fresh perspective on things if you're feeling troubled, especially if it's a sunny day, as sunlight triggers the body to produce mood-boosting Vitamin D.

Besides walking, there are lots of other ways to connect with nature – you could spend more time in your garden, get an allotment and grow your own food, or volunteer with a local conservation group. Research shows that taking part in these activities can improve your mood, ease muscle tension, and positively affect your mental well-being.

OUR GREATEST GLORY IS NOT IN NEVER FALLING, BUT IN RISING EVERY TIME WE FALL.

CONFUCIUS

**The turning point in the process of growing up is when you discover the core of strength within you that survives all hurt.**

Max Lerner

## BUILD YOUR COPING RESOURCES

Mentally strong people recognize they won't be able to combat stress if they're worn out and running on empty. They take regular time out to relax and recharge their batteries.

Consider taking up meditation, yoga, t'ai chi or some other relaxation technique. These activities will help you unwind after a stressful day and help you remain calm during times of stress in the future. Make time to pamper yourself, too – whether that involves curling up on the sofa with a good book or getting a regular massage.

Taking time out isn't self-indulgent; it's an essential strategy for coping with the ups and downs of life. Problems are easier to overcome from a state of relaxation. When we release the tension in our bodies and calm our minds, our creativity and problem-solving skills can come to the fore.

THAT'S ONE THING YOU
LEARN IN SPORTS. YOU
DON'T GIVE UP; YOU
FIGHT TO THE FINISH.

Louis Zamperini

You don't learn
to walk by following
the rules. You learn
by doing, and by
falling over.

Richard Branson

# Tell a
# New Story

While we can't control exactly what happens in life, we can control what we tell ourselves about what's happened. Emotionally robust people have the ability to reframe situations, even when they seem challenging or scary. By looking for value and meaning in stressful events they are able to see "bad" experiences in a positive light. For example, instead of seeing obstacles as stopping you from achieving your goals, you see them as opportunities to adapt and grow.

Instead of fearing failure, you see failure as a necessary stepping stone on the way to success. Reframing is a powerful way to transform your thinking and boost your mental toughness. It won't change the situation, but it will put things into a healthier perspective and keep you motivated to keep going. Try it and see what a big difference it makes.

When you
come to the end
of  your rope,
tie a knot and
hang on.

Anonymous

# IT'S YOUR CHOICE

Mentally strong people take
responsibility for their life. They don't
blame other people for "making
them feel bad" or "ruining their day".
Instead, they take control of their own
thoughts, feelings and behaviour.
They understand that life isn't
always easy or fair, but they don't sit
around feeling sorry for themselves.
Resilient people acknowledge that
everything they do, from the time
they wake up until the time they
go to sleep at night, is a choice.

# Fun Matters

Fun activities are great stress relievers. They give us a zest for life. However, with the responsibilities of adult life, many of us have lost our sense of playfulness.

To introduce more fun into your life, start by writing down what you love doing – going for a bike ride, cuddling your kids, pottering in the garden or learning how to juggle, for example. Next, take a long, hard look at the past week and note how much time you put aside for these things.

The irony is that when we're under pressure we often stop doing the very things that boost our mood and build our resilience. From now on, schedule regular time in your diary to have fun. A great way to recapture your sense of joy is to try something you once loved doing as a kid – you could throw a ball, play a board game, fly a kite or learn a magic trick.

**A little more persistence, a little more effort, and what seemed hopeless failure may turn to glorious success.**

Elbert Hubbard

It's not the winning that teaches you how to be resilient. It's the setback. It's the loss.

Beth Brooke-Marciniak

## GET COMFORTABLE WITH BEING UNCOMFORTABLE

Life isn't easy. We may struggle when we have to move home or experience the loss of a friendship. Strong people accept that change is part of life. They understand that in order for things to improve, they may need to go through some discomfort and uncertainty – whether that's going to job interviews or meeting a financial advisor to sort out their money troubles.

You can build up your resilience by stepping outside of your comfort zone more frequently. Start by trying new things – new foods, new routes to work and so on. If you're feeling more adventurous, you could volunteer in your community, take singing lessons, or learn a new language. Every time you step outside of your comfort zone, you'll increase your tolerance for uncertainty. It may be hard at first but the rewards in the end will be worth it. With uncertainty come new experiences and new opportunities.

WE DON'T DEVELOP COURAGE BY BEING HAPPY EVERY DAY. WE DEVELOP IT BY SURVIVING DIFFICULT TIMES AND CHALLENGING ADVERSITY.

BARBARA DE ANGELIS

**Everyone goes through adversity in life, but what matters is how you learn from it.**

Lou Holtz

## STRUGGLES LEAD TO STRENGTH

The strongest tree in the forest is not the one that is protected from the wind and rain. The strongest trees are the ones that are exposed to the elements. They develop deep roots and stout trunks in order to survive. In the same way, the struggles we face and overcome in life make us stronger. Reminding yourself of this fact can help you weather the storms of life.

Rock bottom
became the solid
foundation on which
I rebuilt my life.

J. K. Rowling

# People Power

It's important to spend time with people who nurture and support you, especially during times of crisis. Being around positive people can uplift you and help you feel less isolated. Friends and family can also act as sounding boards, offering feedback and advice and helping you gain a sense of perspective.

If keeping in touch with your friends has dwindled to the odd email, text or social media post, pick up the phone or arrange to meet for a coffee. Face-to-face interaction helps build trust and brings with it the possibility of hugs and laughter. Laughter triggers the release of endorphins, the body's happy chemicals, and a hug triggers the release of oxytocin, which lowers our blood pressure and reduces stress and anxiety.

Build a community of positive people around you and reach out for help whenever you need support.

SEE ANY DETOUR
AS AN OPPORTUNITY
TO EXPERIENCE
NEW THINGS.

H. Jackson Brown Jr

**It takes no more time to see the good side of life than to see the bad.**

Jimmy Buffett

# FACE REALITY

No one is immune to setbacks. They happen to everyone. The question is, when misfortune occurs, do you waste time and energy resisting what is happening or do you put all your energy into doing what you can to move forward?

If you find yourself regularly thinking things like, "I shouldn't have to deal with this" and "Why me?" you may be fighting reality. Resilient people accept the reality they are faced with, even if it's uncomfortable, and focus all their energy on changing the circumstance or improving their coping abilities.

PERSISTENCE AND
RESILIENCE ONLY
COME FROM HAVING
BEEN GIVEN THE
CHANCE TO WORK
THROUGH DIFFICULT
PROBLEMS.

Gever Tulley

# Keep Calm and Carry On

---

One of the most important keys to resilience during tough times is to control your emotions. It's very easy to get swept away by what is happening and slip into negative thinking. Resilient people are able to remain calm and focused, despite the turmoil that may be surrounding them.

One of the best ways to build this skill is to

practise remaining calm and focused in everyday situations. If you practise on the little things, calmness will become a habit that will kick in when you need it most. The next time you're stuck in a traffic jam or your bag breaks and empties your shopping all over the floor, try remaining cool and calm. The regular practice of yoga, meditation or mindfulness can also help you with this.

**There are plenty of difficult obstacles in your path. Don't allow yourself to become one of them.**

Ralph Marston

# Man never made any material as resilient as the human spirit.

Bernard Williams

# TIME
# FOR BED

Sleep keeps us both mentally and physically strong. Just one night of bad sleep can cause us to feel negative, irritable and more easily overwhelmed the next day. Most adults need at least 7–8 hours' sleep a night but everyone is different.

If you wake up feeling refreshed, you're probably getting enough sleep. If you're not getting enough sleep, the following tips will help: take time to unwind before bed – dim the lights, listen to calming music, have a bath, or meditate. Turn your bedroom into a relaxing space by removing any clutter and painting the walls a neutral, calming colour. Ensure your bedroom is as dark as possible – ban electronic gadgets and consider getting thicker curtains or blackout blinds.

If your mind is racing, try jotting down your thoughts in a diary. These simple actions can turn your bedroom into a peaceful sanctuary and encourage a better night's sleep.

I CAN BE CHANGED

BY WHAT HAPPENS

TO ME. BUT I

REFUSE TO BE

REDUCED BY IT.

MAYA ANGELOU

**Never, never, never give up.**

Winston Churchill

# You can
# do it.

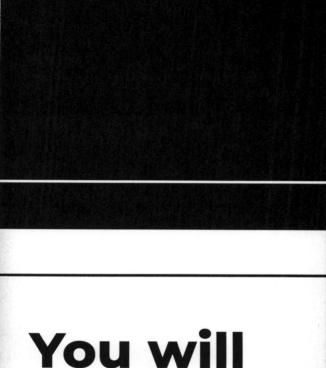

# You will do it.

If you're interested in finding out more about our books, find us on Facebook at **Summersdale Publishers** and follow us on Twitter at **@Summersdale**.

**www.summersdale.com**

## Image credits

pp.4, 5, 12, 21, 25, 32, 33, 42, 52, 63, 68, 77, 82, 85, 91, 92, 105, 132, 133, 143, 148
© Vanzyst/Shutterstock.com

pp.9, 17, 29, 47, 61, 79, 97, 113, 129, 147
© Plasteed/Shutterstock.com